The Tryst

A Call for Relational Intimacy

by
Matt Henning

Bloomington, IN   authorHOUSE®   Milton Keynes, UK

First published by AuthorHouse 9/25/2006

ISBN: 1-4259-6753-1 (sc)

Printed in the United States of America
Bloomington, Indiana

This book is printed on acid-free paper.

All Scripture quotations, unless otherwise indicated, are
taken from the Holy Bible: New International Version. NIV.
Copyright 1973, 1978, 1984 by International Bible Society.

Cover design by Nathan Austin Daniels

This book is dedicated to Campus
Crusade for Christ, Indy Cru.

Contents

A tryst - an assumed designated meeting, freely romantic and without sin - between friend, lover, and Lord. It is out of your control. There will be no idols because your lives will not be like anyone else's. It is a revolution. Your plans, theories, and ideas are thrown away. Your life becomes real.

Introduction

Pick up lines. Pick up lines to me are one of the funniest things ever invented in American culture. You have classic pickup lines, serious pickup lines, and then the "I want to prove I'm not gay" pickup lines.

Classic pickup lines are simple. Your only intention is to make the girl laugh. This is basically you using yourself to tell a joke. No example is needed.

Next there is the serious pickup line. Here you are actually attempting to pick the girl up. An example of this would be like saying "I like your hair like that" or "Your mom is a pretty lady", when what you really mean is "I am saying your hair is nice so you'll talk to me" or "Your mom is pretty which means you are too but I didn't want to just come out and say it".

Finally there is the "I want to prove I'm not gay" pick up lines. These are quite possibly the funniest and most pathetic stories in human history. Here's an example.

The setting is High School. Two guys finished lunch and were just standing by the door when a girl walked out. One guy made a blatant sigh to get her attention while the other followed up by saying "hey girl, do you have a boyfriend?"

Now I am not the coolest person in the world, or the sweetest talker. But you have to think to yourself-first, that's not really that funny so it can't be the classic funny pickup line and secondly I'm pretty sure that's never ever worked in all of human existence! These guys can't possibly think this could've worked. What is she going say? "Hey, no I don't have a boyfriend would you like to be mine?" No! Of course she isn't going to say this! The best guess I could give was that these guys had no female attention and wanted to prove to the world that they weren't gay. I call these "I want to prove I'm not gay" pick up lines. These are funny and entertaining and I'm always up for hearing more of them despite how pathetic they really are. Reason I bring this up now is because they are the best example of people who have no relational intimacy. They have no opposite sex attention, poor relationships, no value on relationships, and really don't know where to start. As funny and sad as it is, in some ways, it's true of all of us. We all in some ways don't understand relational intimacy.

Everyone knows that our relationships with one another are naturally very confusing. We all have opinions and very little biblical evidence to back these opinions up. Dating is even worse. The problem with dating formulas and opinions isn't that dating is wrong- the problem is that it's not the issue. Dating isn't what relationships are about, intimacy is. The real issue with our relationships is intimacy. So to find a pure way of seeking Gods plan in our relationships isn't to study dating, it's to study intimacy.

PART 1

Chapter 1
Intellectual Intimacy

Intellectual intimacy is the deep and personal knowing of one through love. Often times it is connected with deep discussions and personal knowledge of someone.

Awkward...

We've all been here. We get all fired up to hang out with someone and everything is exciting and fun. That first time just seems so great. Then you see them again. Needless to say sparks just aren't flying like they were. Normally you give them the quick answers and you get out as fast as possible.

We've all had our intellectual one night stands too. Were bored and the person we really want to give our attention to isn't there. So we go along with whose around at the time, pretending they're someone else. After it's over, we immediately and purposely forget about them. Truth be told, we've all had to run away from a few boys or girls. And maybe they've run away from us a few times as well.

None the less we know the pains, awkward meetings, and problems of getting to close, to fast or just making a friendship to deep, to soon. We at least know it doesn't feel good for one of us.

> *So the rules are simple with the opposite sex. Don't talk about painful subjects or your never ending problems. Don't hang out to much, don't pray together, and never ever read your bible together. Most of all don't do too much for them at once. The rules of course are there so that we only love our wives and husbands.*

It is my hope that you are choking and gagging. I am.

Cold Fish?

Have you ever met a cold fish? Cold fish are the girls and guys who are normally very upstanding in the Christian circles. They don't date, they don't mess up, and more than anything they don't associate with the opposite sex. They sit only in the girls or guys section, laugh only when the opposite sex isn't around, and if you do by chance talk to them they make you feel more awkward then seeing your parents naked. I know you know what I am talking about. You solve the problem of relational sin by being cold and unloving.

Let me make myself very clear by saying, "God never calls us not to love". Loving to much is not the problem here. I think the problem isn't that we love too much; it's that we do not love enough. So hear me on this. I am not saying its okay to attach yourself to everyone you meet and sit down and have a devotional or prayer time. I'm saying that if you ever think you should love less, you have a wrong idea of what love is.

Chapter 2
Reality of Love

Love makes me laugh. It is good but hurts you? It kills and wakes up your heart? It is no wonder that stupid people know more about it than smart people. It's no wonder that in the end, it confuses us all.

It's a verb. Not an inward but an outward action and feeling. It will push you into action while it stings your nerves and brings chills to your skin. It is an attribute that is always given. It has no human origin but yet we have it. It appears and is given.

Every culture including my own has simplified the word. So many times I hear people say,

"Just love them like those hippies do"

"God is love so everything is okay"

"I know we've only known each other for 1 day but I love you"

If you can identify with the above statements then you are guilty of the same belittling of love that I once was apart of.

The bible speaks of many forms of love- friendship love, romantic love, godly love, etc.

Problem is, we do not communicate as they did. We don't say, "I romantically love you" or "I friendship love you". We just say, "I love you". Furthermore God calls us to love like He does. So we have no need to even think about pursuing any kind of love other than the one He calls us to.

So let me distinguish early on- not by my tone of voice or by actions but rather by these words- Love is either "true love" or "apparent love". Love is always an extremity. If it is less than that, it is a liking not a love.

Apparent Love

Apparent love is in the eye of the beholder and is defined by perception.

Hippies will "love you" as long as you do things the way they like it.

If you hate big business, war, and poverty then your okay, you're just a "loving" person.

But if you hate drugs, sexual immorality, and people who work the system then you are nothing more than an ignorant bigot. There are no truths in apparent love. It's just based upon your perception whether its love or not. You decide. Whatever you think is best. Just try to smile while you're doing it. This is apparent love.

Oprah and Dr. Phil are a great example of apparent lovers. I know most of the world is deeply in love with these people. They are brilliant kind people. It's just that we have to look beyond this. They are like Chameleons. They change colors based on whatever is in front of them. Nothing is real. Just as long as people smile back at them everything is cool and "loving". It doesn't matter if it hurts them in the long run or if it is about them, not God- just so long as people are okay at that very moment. Apparent love means the love is based on immediate pleasures or success.

Others love so they can be rewarded. A Buddhist friend of mine loves so she can get good karma. It isn't for God or for others; it is based on a "give me something" basis. The love is a means to an end of pleasure. So you just "do what you think is right" and I'll "do what my religion says is right" and in the end we all get the most from God. Doesn't matter what God wants, I want what's best for me. This is apparent love.

True Love

True love is circled around truth and is defined and given by God.

The first thing we must realize is that when we call something "true", it must be "truth". Something cannot be true or truthful if it is halfway right. So when I say "true love" it has to be from perfect origin. And since we are not perfect, the first thing we must realize is that WE can never give or become "true love", only God can give and bring it to us. And so we, longing for a glimpse of this true love, must look to Christ.

> 1st Corinthians 13:4-7
> *Love is patient, love is kind. It does not envy, it does not boast, it is not proud. It is not rude, it is not self-seeking, it is not easily angered, it keeps no record of wrongs. Love does not delight in evil but rejoices with the truth. It always protects, always trusts, always hopes, always perseveres.*

Analyzing this verse you see that Paul lays out a few ideals of love. Love is patient and kind and not envious… Being patient is of course hard because you want to have or be where "you" want. Its tough being kind because "you" want what you are seeking. You are envious because "you" want to be better than them.

Everything we do wrong here is because we are looking for the satisfaction of *you*. Everything good that we fail to do we do because we are looking only for the gratification it brings to *you*. If love is not to have anything to do with *you* and to be completely about *others* then as I analyze my life I realize something is wrong. Those feelings I thought were love, were about *me*, not others. It wasn't love. At the same time if loving others is not about seeking my own pleasure than how is it pleasurable? Something doesn't totally make sense.

I think back to the times I've seen 80 year old men opening the doors for their wives or bringing them flowers. They do not want anything in return. Most can't have sex, and I don't mean that sarcastically, it's true. A good gift to an old person is a box of cookies or a cup of tea and that's only if their health allows it. I am not trying to crack on old people; I just want to point out the obvious. Point is that their motives are pretty pure when they are that old and still serving. In essence, they crave seeing the person they love smile. They get their satisfaction from others satisfaction, not their own.

If I were to put this into one sentence it would look something like this.

> *Love is the action, decision, and thought of not pleasing yourself but in turn becoming pleased because you didn't.*

All the while giving God credit for doing the action, decision, and thought through you.

For once it was not about doing or gaining, it was about stopping and giving. No longer could "self-serving" and "true love" be used together. This now is a contradiction and impossibility for these two words to co-exist. If you tell me you "truly love to hate" or you "truly love to sin" or you "truly love to hurt others" I would tell you that is not a true statement. It is a false assumption by society today that they could use such a godly word in such an instance. You cannot love unless you take away your self pleasing. It is simply not possible.

Truly Loving Intellectually

I love the opposite sex. They give me balance. I am masculine and they are feminine. Being around them balances me out. I do not want to be unbalanced, do you? From this I want, need, and should be around the opposite sex. The problem here is not that I want to be balanced or that I am around the opposite sex. The problem is that I make this about me. I make our relationship about what I can get from them. In reality, I do not love them, I love myself.

I have a friend named Sathish Dharma. Sathish could very possibly be the whitest American male that I have ever met. He told me as a child he hung out with all white kids and didn't even know he was Indian. His family isn't Hindu either; he attended a Christian church growing up.

He hates Indian food, the language, and pretty much any other culture that isn't American. However his name is Sathish Dharma and I'm pretty sure that makes him Indian. Despite his obvious ethnic identity issue he is an amazing man of the Lord.

Sathish to me was a master with the opposite sex. He, like all of us, had his moments but for the most part has done pretty well. He goes to the mall with them, serves them, calls them, encourages them, and gets away with it never having someone say he leads them on. He says it's because he's Indian. I disagree. If you really ask him he'd probably tell you, "I make my time about them, not me." He doesn't single any out or look for a best friend or a girlfriend; he just looks out for them. If he likes you, he tells you. Not only does he not single them out but out of "love" he doesn't attempt to get to know them to fast either. Out of love, he doesn't schedule quiet times with them. Out of love, he watches out for them.

Me on the other hand, after I know you for 5 minutes I ask you to come out for coffee. There I ask you deep questions, hear your life story, and whew you with the few topics I'm an expert on. I'm not there for your pleasure, I'm there for mine. I'm not there for friendship or encouragement; I'm there for my pleasure. To me it is annoying having to worry about getting to know them to fast or singling any of them out. I'd much rather not take the time to worry about it. I need their time to make me happy. And so I begin my entire relationship with every girl I know, being self serving.

If we want to love others, we must have discipline. We can't have our one night stands and we can't turn into cold fish. Love is worth the time and annoyance.

Chapter 3
Truth in Love

Love is about truth, not feelings. Love was never meant to be about feelings. It doesn't matter how we feel. You can feel any certain way at any certain time. You can have the same feelings for different situations or not the same feelings in the same situation. It's a confusing paradox.

Love Without Feelings?

Before I thought that good feelings meant the love was real. To say love is about truth just seemed terribly boring. It felt like I was being cheated out of something.

To me love is about passion, excitement, and delight! Many of you can sympathize with me on this. To Say "love isn't about feelings" is like saying, "Don't cry, don't laugh, don't smile, and don't let love affect you". This is not what I am saying.

What I am saying is- discipline and truth don't exactly mean rules or formulas. When we hear truth a lot of us think of the word "law" or control. When I say love is about truth, I am not limiting or giving restraint- I am creating more. I am magnifying the love. Let me explain.

It's like with epic movies. The creative sounds dimmed lighting and chilling music- these things create human emotions, feelings, and a sense of enlightenment inside. Walking out of one of these movies can be such an inspiring stimulating experience. But the next day it's gone. What gives you lasting inspirational experience is realizing that the epic movie is true. Realizing it is true gives passion, excitement, and delight beyond what a simple momentary feeling can come close too. Not only does it magnify it but it brings deep lasting meaning. This is what truth and discipline are- a magnification of those feelings to a greater and deeper level than before. This is why love is about truth.

When we make love about truth, we are simply making it about God. We are giving it to God. God creates and magnifies our appetite for more. Bringing God to your love is bringing life to your love. So bringing truth to love is not killing the feelings and emotions, it is making them stronger.

Why I Am Not a Hopeless Romantic

Why am I not a hopeless romantic? A better question is. Why would I dream about what I see on TV and movies? Why settle for someone else's story or something that a director in Hollywood made up? A Christian should want much more.

God has an imagination much bigger than our own. He is a wonderful artist and creator. Not only does God have a great imagination, but He is writing a story for you. I am not a hopeless romantic because I believe God has a story for me different then the stories others have already lived through- and I don't dream about the movies that a loser director in Hollywood created either.

My friend Russ is known to say some very inappropriate things from time to time. But he also is known to say some very appropriate things. I guess this is the heart and mouth of a passionate person speaking their peace.

He told me once, "You just get lonely and bored and settle for some story that someone else lived through or made up. I think that's pathetic man".

Russ is right. A hopeless romantic is just another word for a pathetic romantic or a faithless romantic. I am not a hopeless romantic. I am a faithful romantic or maybe a foolish romantic. Either way, my love is based on truth, but it is not lessoned, it is magnified. I do not look for a

story someone else made up or lived through. I look for
one new that was created by the greatest writer- God.

Chapter 4
Forgiveness

There comes a point in time when the rubber must hit the road. When your ideals, convictions, and theology has to touch down and move. If your ideals do not cause action then your theology is just banter and it's about you, not God.

Before college I didn't know much about the bible. I didn't even know basic things. While in college I was apart of a movement called Campus Crusade for Christ and started to study- not school work, but the bible. I built my own ideals and I studied theology. Now I know some of you "aren't into theology". You are the type that pulls out the "I just love people" card. I've noticed those are usually the type that will also walk around aimlessly doing good deeds for themselves. Once they lose interest they go to another cause that makes them feel good about themselves.

See when I say I studied theology I meant that I forced my ideals, convictions, and information I learned to mean something to me. It wasn't just knowledge, it became wisdom. Things started to change. Watching the news, reading the newspaper, and reading books about the world all started to mean something to me. I also remembered past events that at the time did nothing to my heart- but now just thinking about them, broke me into tears.

One of those events I still remember to this day as clearly as it happened. It was high school, my senior spring break- San Juan Puerto Rico.

It was a hot day in Puerto Rico. I walked into a scene of bars and tourist shops, the typical vacation area. Just days before I had given my life to the Lord and now things were different. I really had no idea how to act or what to think about things. I just remember thinking that it was in some way wrong what was going on. My friends and I weren't really after the typical vacation anyway so we left that area in search of a restaurant we had heard about from some locals. Most know when you leave the tourist area of a foreign country it's very easy to get lost and sure enough we did. This area of town wasn't exactly dangerous; it was just different- more low key than anything. As I walked around a corner we all laid eyes on a woman sitting on a porch.

I can't really explain this story any other way but to say, she was the most utterly sickening horrid site I have ever looked at. Just looking at her turned my stomach. She had dirty ripped lace up the side of her leg with a bright colored shirt and knotted hair. Cuts and bruises all over her body. I can only describe her face as one that was eroded. I will just end by saying this lady was a prostitute - her life being very different than my own.

I remember being a very young believer not really having ideals and so really all I could do was feel bad for her. So I felt bad for her and forgot about her a few days later. The second time I thought about her was my junior year of college, 3 years later. This time my theology infested into my heart and I realized more about this situation. I started to not just feel bad about her personally, but I asked myself what God feels about her as well.

Does God have a plan for this messed up woman? Does He even care? It's hard for me to conceive what this would look like. If anything happened, I figured it would have to be very small.

What theology shows me here is that it doesn't matter what I think. God says that He does change people, even this lady. God says that He not only could change her, but He wants to regardless of her condition. He also says He wants to change her in big ways. He says we have chances everyday to love people like this and that we need to believe our faith and live it out.

You see how theology which is the study of God goes much further than just some simple feelings? Compassion allows us to want to love them and truth makes us follow through. You see the rubber must hit the road. It is vital we study theology and truth and just as vital we live it out.

Jeremiah 12

Any one of you could probably tell me stories like this. I'm sure you could also come up with many stories of pain and suffering too. Broken hearts maybe, painful memories, and hurtful events- some of you have probably lived through some of these personally.

I am not trying to give you answers to why a loving God allows pain. All I can say is that God gets glory out of everything. I have no answers for you or formulas to make you feel better. I've read some of the books that try and I'm not real into any of that. I'm not sure we are really looking for answers to pain anyway. Take a look at Jeremiah 12. Jeremiah is asking God why good things happen to bad people and why bad things happen to good people. He can't understand the pain. Take a look at verse 5 where God answers. He says, "If you have raced with men on foot and they have worn you out, how can you compete with horses?"

God didn't even answer Jeremiahs question. He simply just asked him about his response. The problem of pain is not that we want to get rid of pain so much as we want to love through the pain. We just want to know how to respond. If we have pain in marriage- the problem isn't the problem, its loving through the problem. If we have pain in a relationship with someone who hurt you- the problem isn't what they did as much as trying to love the person who hurt you because of what they did. The big deal is trying to respond to the thing that hurt you and loving. This is the big problem. Our response is the issue.

Forgiveness

Responding in love to something that hurt you is forgiveness. Loving someone through pain is forgiveness.

By Act of Will?

Forgiveness in our culture is an idea that we "by act of will" make a mends with someone for something they did to us.

I "by act of will" don't do a very good job with this. I "by act of will" never forgive, in fact I can't. You have to realize, I was a disciplined guy. I never got into much trouble, unlike others who messed up all the time. So when they came to me and said sorry or expected me to treat them the same, I wondered why? I was disciplined and good, they were bad.

Now I hated holding grudges. You don't feel good or free when you hold grudges. However I felt cheated, so I held grudges. So simply "by act of will" I didn't do a very good job at forgiving people. I needed more.

To Forgive

I brought my question to my friend Joe. Joe was probably the smartest guy I've ever met. Me and Joe were known to sit up all night for weeks at a time and write bible commentaries. He would read the Greek and tell me what it meant and I'd make it all sound good. During classes me and Joe never studied, we'd always be reading a book or challenging each other with a verse or topic. So I asked Joe before class one day what he thought about forgiveness. He said he'd think about it.

After class I found him nearly in tears. He had spent the entire class writing on forgiveness. Here is the line that stuck out to me most.

"Forgiveness holds both the action and the meaning at once. You are never in the process of forgiving. You may be attempting to love or attempting to hate less but never are you in the process of forgiving. You do it or you don't. You let go or you don't."

Forgiveness has no countertype. You either forgive or you hold the grudge. Holding the grudge is an act of selfishness, you are hording love. Joe is saying that you do not give forgiveness, you either let go or you do not. The meaning and action is one.

What make forgiveness so hard are two things:

One you aren't giving something. Our selfishness wants to give love away- the good feeling or the sense of right. Here we are not giving anything, we are just letting go.

Two if you really forgive someone, then they can hurt you again. If we let go, then we are no longer guarded. Don't lose me here, I am not saying to let people harm you, take advantage of you, or hurt others. I am just saying that when you let go and forgive you can be hurt again because you are trusting again.

Forgiveness is a part of love. Like love, when you forgive someone you are not seeking pleasure for yourself; and in return you gain something. I've learned that what you gain is not exactly what you expect.

Understanding

You receive understanding. You will understand your relationships through forgiveness in a way. You understand your true worth to each other. With the one you love, if they truly love you- then they'll forgive you. If you forgive someone, they understand and really recognize that you value them and not some idea of you.

The day I started to realize this I was having lunch with another friend, Erik. Erik was the type of guy you couldn't describe to others. He had so many confusing attributes. He was smart, funny, athletic, but yet not the normal "good at everything" type of guy. Erik always had interesting ideas. Today we were discussing forgiveness to our future spouses. We always wondered how hard it would be to just look past blemishes and flaws. We were, at the time, dealing with a lot of different "what ifs".

Erik said something really enlightening that day. He said, "Peoples problems are a part of them. If we want to be with them and love them, then we have to accept these things- its part of the deal".

What he meant was, we cannot run away and pretend some things didn't happen. We have to accept what they did and acknowledge that as part of God's plan. With that we simply forgive them because their worth it. We cannot forgive unless we acknowledge what happened and understand the idea that this is a part of the person. We cannot run away from it and pretend the pain isn't there. We have to see people as sinful and not just think of them how we'd like too. They are not some idea, they are people.

People, Not Ideas

Think of all the websites we spend so much time on. We stalk people, Google them, and try to find out everything we can about them and their interests. We eventually find someone who likes all the same things as us and have all the same ideals we have.

Then we meet them and find out their not that great. A good friend once told me, "All the attributes of a person stacked up, doesn't make the person". Meaning all their attributes, the things they like, and the ideals they cling to- isn't all there is to the person. These are just ideas of them, not fully who they are. There is a deeper side we do not see. So with everything, we have to see, feel, and understand their sin and realize who they really are. In turn we have to see our own sin and forgive. Here we can live in the reality of our relationship, not some idea we've made up. Then we can fully love them and understand what they mean to us. If their worth it, then their worth it.

Chapter 5
Conclusion on
Intellectual Intimacy

By now I hope we have realized we are never called to love someone less, but rather to love more. The calling in protecting and experiencing intellectual intimacy is not to withhold love; the calling is to love to the tips of your bodies.

Intellectual intimacy can appear to have many grey areas. We are called to take on these grey areas by pursuing truth. With intellectual intimacy the answer is simple. Just love them to the fullest. This is the beauty and simplicity of intellectual intimacy. Just love them and this means making the relationship about them, not you.

The beginning and end of all intellectual intimacy is love. We must obey the calling to love not halfway, but all the way.

PART 2

Chapter 6
Emotional Intimacy

Emotional intimacy is the acknowledgment of the truth of your relationships and the feelings that result. In other words, it is not an attachment, false pleasure, control, an addiction or based on feelings. It is the feelings and emotions that come from the acknowledgement of truth- of what your relationship is.

Emotional intimacy is the magnification of truth that brings about a longing, anticipation, or a satisfaction. You long to spend time with the Lord when you acknowledge His greatness, your weakness, and His love for you anyway. The magnification of this truth triggers your longing for Him and it also increases your satisfaction when you feel Him around you or when He blesses you. This is the emotional part to intimacy- the acknowledgement of truth and the authentic "real" feelings that stem from it.

We cannot rely on feelings, we rely on truth. However, anyone who says they seek and find truth but no feeling come from this- never found truth. Truth is meant to put us on our face, to stun us, and to fill us with a passion for life. If you aren't a passionate person, then you have not found or acknowledged truth.

Emotional intimacy to me is the key part of growth in a relationship. A healthy relationship is obviously one that is always seeking God and while most relationships do seek God, only some acknowledge the truths of God. Like who and what He is in their relationship. I think the true growth in a relationship happens when you both together realize who and what you are to God- both individually and together as a couple. This process will in turn bring about a longing for each other, anticipation for more, and a satisfaction in what God is and has done in your relationship. This is called emotional intimacy because it will break about emotions, feelings, and deep passion.

The Acknowledgement

The acknowledgement is this. That God is not only apart of your relationship, but is what your relationship is about. This is dazzling.

Chapter 7
Soul-Mates

Wolverine Peak: Anchorage, Alaska

It was 5pm trying to make it to the top by 10pm, a 5 hour window. This was only about an 8 mile hike and we thought if we stopped for no breaks we would make it.

Following the path of devil's clove (poisonous leaves) it soon grew narrow. We started seeing the wild animals and smelling the nature around us.

We crossed through hot springs and the heat rose up our legs. As the mountain got steeper we saw the most amazing pictures of the city of what seemed only a few feet away. Suddenly as I turned the mountain cliff there was a young man sitting on the ground Indian style reading a book. His glare later made me realize, he was more stunned to see us up there then we were to see him.

His name was Raven. A Raven had flown from the sky and landed on his shoulder, or so he claimed. It was an eerie night and we all had similar feelings like maybe we'd be robbed, shot, or killed.

I was the first up the turn and half-startled, half confident I asked how he was. He didn't say good or bad but rather he asked me why my back-pack was so big. He wondered what need it was for. After a little bit of badgering of my backpacking choices he asked us if we knew a man. We recognized this man as a big leader of a Satanist organization. He told us that was what he practices. We briefly answered and then asked him if he knew God. After a few minutes of useless banter a question arose, we asked him if he had hope. His first answer was "no, none". We said, "how about a family?" He said he was homeless, a mountain man. We asked him what had happened but little would he answer. We asked him again, "You have to have some hope. What is it? It can be big or small."

He turned reached for his neck and lifted up a necklace around his neck. He said, "This is my hope".

It was a necklace with a ring around it. I believe the one he had given his ex-wife. The conversation drastically turned and he could no longer say life was not worth living, because in fact he had hope. The single greatest trigger a human mind can concept hit him. It was the idea of love; the bridge now between a Satanist and a Christian and the bridge now between a homeless mountain man and a bunch of well off Christian men. We talked that night; Raven was at the least exposed to Christ and real love. After a 2 hour delay Raven finished Wolverine Peak with us. He was the first to reach the top; we spent the early morning with him eating and drinking together atop the peak.

But that's not the end of the story. Raven said something that night that I still cannot forget. When he lifted the necklace around his neck and declared his hope, he called it- "the ring for his soul-mate". He wanted a friend and he called it his "soul-mate".

I've always been shocked at how easily non-spiritual people will fall into using such spiritual words. I guess it's pretty dim-witted to ask why love causes a man to see and feel spiritual things. However at the same time, I find it interesting the most common spiritual thing that most unspiritual people talk about is soul-mates. They don't believe in God but believe God brought them there wife or husband. It's absurd and funny and at the same very interesting. What makes man and woman think so deeply about this   foolish theory?

Soul-Mates

I will just start out by saying that my friends and I believe this very foolish concept. We agree with Raven. We believe in soul-mates. We are deep thinkers and have all come from different theological backgrounds. Yet we are all convinced by scripture and plain reason that not only do soul-mates exist but that it is completely vital that everyone accept this theory. Here's why.

Acknowledgement as I said before is what brings about emotional intimacy because it gives us truth. Truth is so beautiful and elite that it brings about real true emotions that do not fade away like short-lived feelings but yet endure through and through. The truth of God being not just a part of your relationships, but being about your relationships is the greatest truth you can acknowledge.

Reason with me- the one thing you do not want to give up is your relationships. You can give God your life, money, ministry, and mostly all else. For most, your lives are about serving God, your ministry is about God, and your money is about God. I just notice to most people relationships don't apply. We think our spouses are a gift to us as if they still aren't for God? We think their, for us. We never imagined that maybe who we marry is not about us, but maybe about what God wills for us to do.

And so the greatest acknowledgment is that not only is God a part of our relationships, but He is what our relationship is about. Everything was created by God's will, for God's will(Rev. 4:11).

I know some people are married right now and they might be thinking that they married the wrong person and not doing God's will. They believe that they chose to marry someone and it was the wrong choice. So not only did God lose, but so did "they". "They" lost, "they" lost for God, "they" messed up their relationship and there is no going back. Do you see the theme? It is once again about them. Their relationship was never acknowledged to be about God, he was just a part of it.

So to begin, we must first realize two things. One that God never loses and secondly that not only is God a part of our relationships, but is what our relationships are about.

Soul-Mates Defined

At my school believing in soul-mates was a good way of getting a date. I can remember talking about it with a girl once and her boyfriend said he didn't believe in it. They broke up a short time later. It's true that nobody wants to be in a relationship with someone that doesn't completely believe they are a part of a bigger plan of Gods. So I knew what I wanted to believe. They only thing left was to find out if what I wanted to believe was right. I had to start with defining what a soul-mate even was.

-Lost halves: Some believe we are condemned to spend our lives searching for the other half of ourselves. Meaning, our lives are centered on a pursuit to find a certain person. This is an absurdity that God "would call" anyone to spend their lives looking for someone else. My calling in life is to find someone? This could possibly be the most dimwitted of all ideas.

-Reincarnated lovers: Buddhists believe we are reincarnated beings that we knew from previous lifetimes. I'm inclined to believe my soul was created by God and will be given to Him at death. I guess since I do not believe in reincarnation the answer is simple. For those who do I'd simply ask, "What happens when someone has reached nirvana? What happens to their other half if they haven't yet reached nirvana?"

-Kindred Spirits: This is the idea that there is someone like us that we either marry or become good friends with- whichever we choose. In this theory a God creates someone for us, but then stops halfway and lets us either marry it or be friends with it. It doesn't matter what His will was for creating it! This is funny, yet a lot of people believe this too.

-Lottery picks: Here is the belief of the majority of Christians. You marry anyone. Like the lottery, you are roaming around the earth and whatever ball pops up, you see your similarities, have a little fun together, go to

church a few times, and poof you're married. All joking aside, this belief holds that there are a few handfuls of people who would make you happy. Based on your free choice you pick the one you run into first or like most at the time. This belief seems logical at first site but when closely analyzed you see the common trait. God's will is not in the equation. You are the focus of it.

When things cease to be about God they become radically wrong. This is exactly what is happening here. The intimacy of a relationship becomes about what we choose and have fallen into and is no longer about what God wills or about what His plan entails. If you believe any of the theories above, you will not have true intimacy. There is only one theory that can ever give you true intimacy. That is the biblical ideal theory of soul-mates. A God given love story, that suffers through pain and hardships, to receive the exact person who God created for you to be with- all for the glory of God.

We are not condemned to spend our lives searching for the other half of ourselves. We are not reincarnated beings that we know from previous lifetimes; our souls are for God and are given to God at death. It's not about our own earthly connection nor is it a friend with strong bonds. It's not about probability or work-it-out theories. Soul-mates are what you are, not what you become.

-Biblical Soul-mate: The person God has ordained for you before the creation of the world. It is the person, who is or at one time was placed on a winding painful joyful road headed straight for you. It is what you are, not what you become. A soul-mate is God created. He is the author, creator, and story-teller. Our soul-mate is not for us. They are not meant as a gift either, although they truly are. Simply you walk in the will of God together. You live and breathe for the glory of God and your greatest pleasures lie in the pursuit of this.

Objections

There are of course objections. Many have asked me over the years about those who are divorced and remarried- which were their soul-mate. Many like to also point out that a lot of people who are married hate each other. Then there are singles who never get married.

These objections raised have not only been taken into account by others, but they are naturally accepted. There are no biblical examples and God's character completely refutes this, but still they are just blindly taken for granted as fact.

I will admit these questions have stumped me for some time. At one point I gave up and said I didn't believe any longer either. I said, that I didn't care what the bible said nor what God's character tells me, these objections were just too much to deal with. Then God spoke to me. I realized I had always judged things based on success. It was about our earthly perspective, not truth.

God's Choice for Hosea

Things had to be turned around. In Hosea we see an example where God chose Hosea to marry a whore. God not only chose Hosea to marry her but He also called Hosea to passionately pursue her heart even though he knew she wouldn't remain faithful. Hosea loved her and had a family with her, even through all the hurt and pain. I admit, this isn't the relationship I want and it's my guess you feel the same way. Point is the relationship isn't about success or perspective. The relationship is about God and what He wants.

I want to be careful because I have no idea who is reading this. It is not okay to be unfaithful or to be okay with unfaithfulness. In fact it is despicable to do anything but long for purity with your husband or wife. The point is that beyond this God gets glory out of all pain and at the same time we receive wisdom through it.

Solomon's One

Solomon is another great example I believe. He had many wives. Maybe this is like those who remarry after being widowed. This could also be like divorce although

I am not saying anything about divorce except that it is wrong. None the less, Song of Solomon is a tale of this "one" person whom he treated above all else- one he wined and dined and loved and pursued. He loved her wit, purity, and beauty. He gave his heart to just her, thought endlessly about her, and she made him want to be a better person. Even Solomon who had hundreds of wives- set one apart.

Singles

The hardest question to answer with soul-mates is to single people. My simple answer is that God isn't punishing them or giving them less of a plan. They were chosen to share their souls only with God. They have been given knowledge and understanding that couples will never receive. I do not have any formula I just know that Paul describes this as better.

Who belongs to who or who is destined for what are questions we can never answer until they happen. It isn't that there isn't an absolute answer; it's simply that we are not meant to know, control, or create it.

I don't know who is faking Christianity and who is saved. Just the same I don't know whose soul-mate is whose. All I know is that when God brings you together with someone in intimacy you need to acknowledge His control over it and His complete sovereignty in it. Most of all do not take a single ounce of credit for it. See it as God's divine act and live like you believe it is true- because it is. If you are single, believe the same. It was God.

Chapter 8
Your Friend and Story

A Desire

Since I was a boy when I peered at girls it was a scenario I played in my head time after time. I loved it so much. It was that I would make this friend and at first we would just like each other purely; and then after time we would both at the same time realize that we loved each other. We would grow up together and be *meant* for each other. I had such great desire for this simple thing that deep down I would do anything for it to be. I would sin, lie to myself, and hurt others. Basically subconsciously I would do anything to have this relationship.

And I guess whatever you thirst for; you can in time, turn something into this. We compromise in our minds. We make up the fantasy we'd always longed for and tie it into something we've already got or had.

Meaning we have a desire or longing for something. Something we want so much that we will actually invent something that seems like this desire in order to fulfill it.

I digress.

High School Idealism

My friends often talk about high school, even if they hated it, like it was a different time in their life. I guess just something about it was unique. My first couple years of college I would come back and look at photo albums. The zealous pursuit of things that made my life so great then- it was reckless, and passionate. Oh and the girls I knew I found the greatest memories in. We knew nothing about the other but just stumbled into friendship.

I found mystery in all the friendships I sought after knowing/thinking they would never let me down. I found great restoration and peace knowing that God loved me so much and that I could do anything and really not worry about Him messing up, just extreme pursuit of God.

The younger days are so remembered because it was a time of innocence. You ran the night unnoticed and you did whatever your heart desired. You lived in high school or maybe for some of you it was college- and you still long for guys or girls who can represent this.

You see, we don't fully know ourselves or other people. We haven't yet realized that people will let us down. The seriousness of our actions hasn't plagued us quite yet. We do not fear failure in the way we will.

We want high school or younger days because then things would be idealistic again. We could then run around being Nobel and not caring, not hiding, and not having to worry about the other person tricking us; rather we would do the right things with pure hearts because we think people are "good".

Here's the crazy thing too. While you live like this people are still able to get to know the real you. For one, you are growing and getting to know yourself which is a special time, but you are also open to letting everyone inside.

And for that person you care about most then, they will walk inside. Good or bad, they are coming in. Someone or something has too.

So no matter who you are, no matter where you've been. Everyone's life is still the same. Whether it was a relationship of 4 years, 4 months, 4 weeks; or a crush of 4 years- the reality is the same. More than likely while you got to know yourself, someone else did too.

With this person there is a peace and security in them knowing everything about you and growing with you. This is a time you are completely open. It's wonderful and exciting; fast paced and intense. And like all good things, it comes to an end. The ending isn't a bad ending though, its reality.

This Love

Man can hurt when he has nobody to love, but he can only truly feel pain when he has somebody he cannot love. The hurt of losing this person or thing is almost too hard to describe in words- it just hurts.

They know everything about you. Not the secrets, not the real person you could become. But they have lived when you lived and this to you is beautiful, it commands your heart.

And this feeling isn't wrong. We as people want a person who we can share ourselves with, an open box. But we want to be secure and we want to be real. We don't want to hide ourselves. We want to lay open showing all of us, and for them to love this.

Think of the problems you'd go through just to be understood. We'd go to the ends of the earth just to tell a girl we want to be the strongest person in their life. And women, well you'd go to the ends of the earth, just to be seen deeply by someone.

And so we long, dream, and desire.

Then when it doesn't work out we settle, fail, and die.

We grow up things change and relationships fade. However, some people don't fade away.

We are left asking this world and God many questions. What is this person and why won't they leave my head? It seems they will never go away? I hate more than anything seeing people in this un-needed pain. This to me is the life of most people, including myself. We think our chance is gone. We think it's too late.

Luckily it doesn't matter what we think. God's perspective is what is real and true. So we must see this pain and longing for what it is.

Addiction

This is nothing more than an addiction. Simply, it is something you have become dependent on, a habit. Something you have found to be great, made to think it is something much greater, and now depend upon. An addiction uses something that is good but never stays. It brings great feeling but never fulfillment, just more obsession.

One friend met her first real great Christian guy at summer camp in the middle of high school. It was her first kiss and also first real connection with someone who was pure and real with her. Later they broke up. She would date other guys, think of him, and break up with them soon after. One guy she broke up with because she heard his radio show that night. She looks back now with a smirk and wonders what she was even thinking. I relate with this story a lot. We've all been there with feelings that seem like they'll stay forever. Later we realize there just fleeting addictions to the ideas of people, not reality.

Another friend dated his girlfriend all through high school. Was deemed "best couple" senior year- only now to break up. I spoke to him while he was in college and he said the only thing that makes sense to him is their relationship. Not her, but their relationship. They were both addicted.

Sometimes these people really are good for the other. They excite each other, the relationship is healthy and pure, and God is the true focus. They long to serve Him together and pursue Him with everything. A relationship should be these things. If it is, then it is good. If it is not, then know it is an addiction. An addiction that is not real.

Generic vs. Authentic

Now this longing, which is felt by everyone in some way is bigger than what you think; with great meaning behind it, good pure meaning.

All addictions are a generic form of something else. When you have something generic you must also have something authentic. You can't have a remake unless something has already been made. You can't have a fake person, unless there is already a real person. Having something generic or a short stack of something else is proof that there is also something authentic and real.

For instance, Lust; we are meant to have beauty but we accept Lust. We want adventure but settle for drama. We want comfort and love but get weary and become drunk. We want to lead and help but instead become control freaks.

Just like with medicine, why buy the real stuff when you can get the generic brand cheaper?

We do this with our love. Sooner or later we can't even notice a difference.

Addictions are the easy way out of something greater. There is an authentic side.

So what is the authentic part of this addiction?

Innate inside each one of us we desire more than anything something "divinely given" to us. We don't want to choose it; we want it to just "come to us". That is why with these people we look for signs- we ask questions like,

"Why is this person in my life so early?"

"Why would they just be here in my life at this time?"

"Why did I experience this with them, if we are not meant to be?"

We use words such as- signs, fate, destiny, fortune, chance, luck. As if something in the universe is coercing the process. This isn't that far off either. It's just there is more to it.

> *Our addiction is proof that a divinity is compelling you towards someone special. Put bluntly, our addiction is just more proof that soul-mates exist.*

Think about it. Why do people just naturally love the words fate and destiny in context to relationships? Why do romantic comedies use words like fate and destiny to spark our interest? There is something that we are born with- a certain longing and desire. We of course "try" to make our relationships look like the movies we watch or the things we want but this is just a cover up for something deeper. We were born to want something more.

Inside these addictions lay some sort of truth that is trying to tell us something. It is telling us of a divinity or work of a God that is somewhat controlling the surroundings. Something we are not in control of. Some would say this is proof of soul-mates and from a basic philosophical perspective I would have to agree.

Still the Problem

Instead of going to God, asking him to take you there. We instead go there and then go to God. We control the intimacy of the spirit. We once again panic, control the situation, take ourselves to the person we have chosen, and make them into this being. It once again takes us back to the generic love.

Don't be fooled, this generic love isn't so bad. Love is such a strong trigger to us that even the generic feeling of it is beyond wonderful- at the time.

So we settle, compromise, die, give up, harden, run away, stop thinking, stop trying, and cry.

Sacrificing Isaac

I remember the day I asked God to take control. I emailed a famous author of a book that was very important to me. I explained my dilemma. I told him I couldn't give her up, it just wasn't my decision, and my heart wouldn't let me. Much to my surprise he wrote back. He said my story was much like his.

He went on to say, "This sounds like a sacrificing Isaac" deal- As if he's dealt with this a million times before.

Abraham, as you remember, was told to slaughter his young son for the Lord. Abraham agreed and tried but the Lord came back and stopped his hand. He sacrificed it to God and God gave it back to him. Many say this passage shows Abrahams trust in God's promise. Either way, the point is to trust God's promise to be in control of our lives. It was about a sacrifice to God and if it was God's will, He will bring it back.

This famous author believed this was something God loved to do. He confessed to me that it probably will not work in my favor like Abraham. Naturally, I was hopeful none the less that it would, I believed it would; and eventually I found out that it not only wasn't going to happen, but that I didn't want it to anymore.

I mean the girl I liked was not a bad girl. She was wonderful. We had great times and she was very godly. It however was not my story, not my perfect story that God had written Himself. I know this now, I did not then. I now am glad it didn't work out but I can tell you honestly, I was not glad then. Luckily God knows how we will feel down the road even though we do not. Surrender is hard, but it's good.

Surrender

The pain didn't just instantly go away. Things continued to creep and slither into my life everyday. People thinking I was crazy, saying that the vision I have is unreasonable, and more so telling me that I was just being super spiritual- making God into this fairy tale.

Surrender is not just saying you won't date or think about the opposite sex anymore. It isn't dating every new person you meet either. And you can't just run away from things. Surrender is about believing the truth that God is speaking. Believing the ideas that God is most important and that He is most fulfilling and that He is in control. You have to believe these ideas and not just be inactive. Ask Him to bring you your story and wait for it.

A common pessimistic phrase I heard often was, "I'm not cynical I just put things in perspective". From looking at the great people of faith I have realized that putting things in perspective is no better than denying and cursing God, limiting him to his full love and power.

When I decided to begin my quest for authenticity and to sacrifice my life to God's will and plan, I had to give up more than I thought. I had to give up my pragmatic ideas and learn to live as an idealist. Living this way was not natural to me.

An Idealist

If I were to describe idealism I'd have to introduce you to my friend Nate. Imagine a guy who is 70 years old sitting in a chair smoking a pipe- as he is smoking his pipe he is telling stories of how he went to foreign lands, almost died, found secret treasure, and wrote wonderful stories about it. Now imagine what he would look like when he was 20. This was Nate.

Nate, like all of my friends, had a similar story to me. He had great wisdom in what surrender looked like. To him it was character.

While good character was not perpetual to me, I still tried. I found it was okay to be ideal, disciplined, and to give into my own desires- to go to God first, and to let him lead me to this place. Nate stressed discipline in all areas of life- to sweat things out sometimes.

I worked at this discipline and wouldn't let false anticipation take over my life. I wouldn't let it be my source of hope. I let God be my hope. I blindly believed in His revealing of whatever I was to receive.

This is one of those times when it is easier said then done. I can attest to this. But I can also say that I made it through and so did Nate, and Joe, Erik, Russ, and Sathish. We have all been through it together and we all made it out. We now look back and see why we desired what we did. We acknowledge now that this was just a good part of our hearts trying to get out. That what we desired was a God appointed love story. Now all that's left was waiting- and believing. So we waited, and believed.

We write this and tell you about our lives not because it is the most successful way- We tell you this because it is the right way.

Chapter 9
The Creator of our Story

Some choices we must admit are not choices. Were you given the choice to be Indian, African, or English? Weren't some born with a full head of hair, some born bald? Some born male, some born female (and I have done research- everyone, even at an early age, can be classified male or female)? There are innate things that leave us with no choice.

Now sin brings upon confusion. I know this. But I can speak for myself. I do not have a free choice. I am attracted to women, I love the taste of steak, and the smile of a girl and the smell of the outdoors uncontrollably makes my heart burn with desire. I didn't make myself love steak and women. That would be like saying I could make myself love anything. I do not love coconut nor could I ever make myself- I think coconut is disgusting.

I can't choose to dislike steak and women, because I love them. I just do.

These loves I didn't choose, they chose me. And so it is with everything we love. We just love them- and it's about them, not us. We do not choose what we love, they choose you.

Joe my smart friend called me one day laughing. He said "I just saw the funniest commercial on TV"

I asked "what Joe, what now".

He said, "It was a carpet commercial."

"Sweet Joe" I answered.

"No, you don't understand" he said, "listen it said, do you choose to be inspired or does inspiration choose you. Come to so and so carpet store and let our carpet inspire you!" He continued, "The carpet just takes your breath away right? It's not your choice you just are inspired by the carpet!"

"What's your point Joe" I said.

"You don't get it" he continued again "you don't choose! Your just inspired without control over the inspiration, it chooses you!"

I usually laugh at Joe's little soapboxes but this time he was right. Carpet sadly does inspire some people but this wasn't what he meant.

Let's use this in context to a relationship. Sometimes the opposite sex just takes your breath away. You realize

everything about them and they just "take your breath away". Sometimes it's not that systematic either, you just like them. You didn't "choose" to like them, you just did. In a sense, they do choose you.

To me it is reasonable to say that to become anything but what God willed for you is as silly as a woman thinking she can somehow make herself into a man. Castration won't do this; other materials cannot do this- deep inside of you lies something that cannot lie. No I'm not talking about a uterus or other things men do not have or a sperm sac that women cannot have but a soul that God deemed one or the other. It is a body and soul which in the completion of heaven will be fully restored to its perfect form, age, and state. This clay belongs to God.

What is God in Control of?

Many people ask me was Mary given the choice to be the mother of Jesus or did it just happen? Were the Egyptians given the choice after 7 plaques to give up and let the Jews go or would there need to be an 8th? And what would the 8th plague have been, since the greatest of the Egyptian gods was mocked on the 7th plaque? Were the writers of the New Testament allowed to write falsities, could they if they wanted too? Was it just "luck" that they all wrote complete truth- or was there something else at hand?

I often ask my friends if I had a lemon, orange, or apple in my fruit basket which they would "choose". Most of my friends are particularly fond of oranges. So once in awhile, to make the trick fun I only put a lemon and apple underneath. When they chose the orange I uncover the basket only to have a lemon and apple. I tell them that there is a bug that got loose and the oranges went bad and there were no longer any oranges at the store. Because of this I was unable to buy any. So I ask them, which do you choose now? They take the apple usually. I give them the apple and I ask, "Did you really choose the apple? Or was this choice based upon what was determined before hand? Did nature change your choice and so was it really a free choice away from anything else at all? Of course it wasn't "free". Simple human perception makes us believe a lot of nonsensical ideas. We just have to realize they simply are not true.

Chapter 10
What God Says

In the end, nothing matters except for what God says-even if its explanation cannot be explained by you. Truth in the end is the only thing that matters and Scripture is where we find truth.

My Soapbox

A hot topic for me is justification by faith alone. I believe that salvation must be seen as a gift from God, by faith alone. If anyone disagrees with me and says it's not by faith but by works, I ask them what it would take for them to agree with me. Most would say, "Prove it to me with Scripture".

If I told you that Scripture said "you are saved by faith alone, not by works and it is a gift from God" then you'd agree with me? Most would answer yes. Then I would simply point out Ephesians 2: 8-9.

Ephesians 2:8-9
"For it is by grace you have been saved,
through faith—and this not from yourselves,
it is the gift of God— not by works, so that
no one can boast."

It's pretty clear. Now throughout this section I have made many assumptions and claims about Soul-mates and the creating sovereign control of God. So I ask you now, what will it take for you to agree with me?

He determined exactly where people live and when they live there (if your married then you'd have to acknowledge you were both put in the same place at the same time by God)

Acts 17:26
"From one man he made every nation of
men, that they should inhabit the whole
earth; and he determined the times set for
them and the exact places where they should
live."

He wrote down and ordained every day of your life before one day occurred.

Psalms 139:16
"your eyes saw my unformed body.
All the days ordained for me
were written in your book
before one of them came to be."

God's plan is the one that occurs, not yours.
> Proverbs 16:1
> *"To man belong the plans of the heart,*
> *but from the LORD comes the reply of the*
> *tongue."*

Whatever God wants to happen, happens.
> Proverbs 21:1
> *"The king's heart is in the hand of the*
> *LORD;*
> *he directs it like a watercourse wherever he*
> *pleases."*

God works in you to will and to act in accordance to His purpose.
> Philippians 2:13
> *"for it is God who works in you to will and*
> *to act according to his good purpose."*

God's promise is irrevocable
> Romans 11:29
> *"for God's gifts and his call are*
> *irrevocable."*

God wins every time
> Proverbs 21:30
> *"There is no wisdom, no insight, no plan*
> *that can succeed against the LORD."*

Stars aren't even out of God's control. God determines the number and knows each by name.

> Psalms 147:4
> *"He determines the number of the stars and calls them each by name."*

Not one thing happens apart from the will of the father.

> Matthew 10:29-31
> *"Are not two sparrows sold for a penny? Yet not one of them will fall to the ground apart from the will of your Father. And even the very hairs of your head are all numbered. So don't be afraid; you are worth more than many sparrows."*

There are only so many verses I can give you before this becomes monotonous. Every page of the bible is flooded with this same theme. God is not just superior in our life, but His will happens in even the smallest of things.

Do Not Remain Blind

Once I was debating a religious topic. My friend showed me biblically where I was wrong. He not only proved it, but he proved it overwhelmingly. I admitted I was wrong and walked away. My other friend sitting next to me said, "Even though you showed me biblical proof

I just choose not to agree". Russ was sitting there and he said, "I love it when people choose to remain blind." I laughed at the time but I always remember it when I'm studying Scripture. If it says it, it's true.

I plead with you guys. Do not disregard the bible, plain reason, and your hearts. It is very clear. Do not remain blind. You must trust in what is foolish to the world to see what is perfect in the kingdom. Do not remain blind.

PART 3

Chapter 11
Physical Intimacy

The final part of intimacy is physical intimacy. Physical intimacy is the action that stems from intellectual and emotional intimacy infusing in such great abundance that it overflows and becomes physical.

Spirituality is pure. And so it goes without saying that intellectual, emotional, and physical intimacy must be from a pure source as well. It also must be established to be carried out with complete purity.

It is true that people are physical with others without emotional or intellectual intimacy. This action is not physical intimacy- it is sin. It is a false bond, a generic love, and a fake emotion. I am not just blaming non-religious people of this sin either. I am blaming most Christians today.

Accepting Lust

There's a funny story I tell from time to time. I was younger and we were having bible discussion. The question arose, "what do you want in your future wife?"

The answers were obviously cliché. Some had a list of things; others just said someone normal and down to earth. It got around to me and half alert I just said, "I want a girl who is nice, cute, caring, on fire for God, and a slut in bed".

When I tell the story in person it gets a laugh and when I said it in the room it got a laugh and everyone agreed. I can't say this any other way though. While funny, and also sadly while most agree - what I said was wrong, and degrading.

Physical intimacy is less of a physical thing and more of a spiritual thing. I need to be turned on by her beauty, not my lust. I need to let my love and spirituality magnify the pleasure and not sell it short by making it about me. Lust is self-seeking and so it is not love.

The organization or church building most Christians attend, give rules. If you're married, all is okay or you can kiss just be dating for a good while first. Sadly, most of you would agree with these statements. I however do not. I believe these rules are no less sinful than a one night stand or a random party hook-up. Both are impure. Both in the end seek their own gratification. The love is not for the other. Their lives are not acknowledged to be completely for God. Their physically intimacy is not from the source of God.

When we look at the ideals of God, we see a different story of a pure relationship. Marriage is not a go ahead to gratify yourself, it is a covenant promise acknowledging what God wants and promising your true love to each other. Dating isn't a timeline to be physical; it is a journey leading up to the promise. I am not here to tell you when it is okay to do what or when you should be married or what you should do with your life. I don't know God's plan for you. Truth is, I never will.

So let's stop believing the lies. Let's stop reading the 10 basic steps to a perfect dating relationships or a "hurry and get married" philosophy. Let's follow God's design for holiness. Let's love in our relationships and acknowledge God as creator. Let us tell the flesh that were through- Let us magnify God with His holiness.

Chapter 12
Believe

One of the saddest things I experienced while in college were listening to the people, who came to me saying,

"I have lost the chance of having something special"

"My mistakes have ruined any chance of a pure relationship"

"My story can never be felt to the extent others will"

"I am not good enough"

"God doesn't care"

These are the feelings of so many people. They feel like they missed their only chance of either meeting the right person or waiting on that person.

Most of this is because people have felt some type of bond with someone and they think they will never love again. Or that they have already experienced everything about love and the chance is over. Some believe God simply doesn't care or that their sin was too much.

We forget what true love is. We think intimacy is just some bond, fake or not. Marriage means we don't sin anymore. Forgiveness is words muttered. Truth is relative. Intimacy is subjective. We think God doesn't care.

These words are horrific, unbiblical, and illogical. They are not the words of God. If you are experiencing this, I understand. But in the same breath I have to say you believe something that is wrong. We have just gone through intellectual, emotional, and physical intimacy. We have learned the truths. So don't believe the lies. Acknowledge the truth and trust in God regardless of the pain. He must be believed in.

Our Response

I always ask my friends the question. It all begins with an arranged marriage. You have 3 choices of a future spouse. The first is very ugly, very ungodly, and very mean. The second is average. Not just by looks, but she is average in her spirituality and average in her personality. The third is very beautiful, very god-loving, and very perfect for you.

A man pulls out a coin and says, "you can either have the average one or you can flip this coin. If it lands on heads, you get the 1st girl. If it lands on tails, you get the 3rd girl."

Which do you choose? To have the average person for you or do you take the chance?

I never said things were easy. In fact I am not telling you to do what is easiest or the way that is successful. I am telling you to do what is right. I'm flipping the coin. I believe the coin was created by God. That the breeze that pushes it and the finger that flips it was created by God also. I believe its staged. Not only do I believe its staged but I trust that God was in control of my past and in control of my future- that God wants whats best for me. I live like I believe this and I flip the coin.

Chapter 13
Feeling

Sensitization to Purity

After spending days in the wild, little things start happening to your senses. You become aware of things. You learn to hear an ant, to smell the water in the river, you feel the animals walking. Native Indians knew this. They lived apart from us this way. They could hear and smell the actions. However there was nothing special or magical about their ears or noses. Simply, their senses were in touch with reality.

This is the same with right and wrong, peace and love. They aren't things we can learn to hear, learn to see, and find to know and understand. They are things we bring ourselves back too. We knew the way long ago. These things are deep in our hearts and through the spirit they can be found again. This comes through sensitization.

Many girls tell me, whatever you do, don't put your arm around their stomach. They say it is a very sensitive thing. Like us boys, the knee up is off limits.

I know both men and women in ballet. On a daily basis they practice "lifts" and "turns". This of course means their stomach will be touched. At the end of the day, touching their stomach is no big deal. But do it to a girl who isn't in ballet and you may find that the same rules don't apply. This is because touch here has been desensitized. From its original way, things are different.

Point here is not that ballet is wrong. These friends of mine are wonderful godly women. This is an example of something being desensitized from its original way.

Desensitized Culture

I was always pretty serious with my ministry. I devoted a great amount of time to it. I went to church 4 times a week, did numerous outreaches, shared my faith, discipled others- and still went home and watched ridiculous stuff on TV. So what is the difference? Some go out in public and wear tight clothing, others watch it on TV. Some have sex, others watch it on TV. We all give into this sex culture in some way. We have all desensitized ourselves from true purity. You know its sin, but decide it's not as big of deal to God. Some evangelize, do outreaches, care for others and do these things to replace purity.

We as a culture have not missed this. We as a culture simply do not care. Our standards are gone. Some post-modern churches teach that holiness doesn't matter as long as we have faith. That we can watch trashy movies as long as people come to church. As long as things work, it's worth doing them. In a sense we are saying that God cannot break through our culture without committing sin. That we cannot get through to non-believers unless we compromise- that we need the sex culture. Once again, even though we know what is right, we are too desensitized to believe it.

Then we wonder why we are so disillusioned to reality. Why things stop making sense to us. We settle and then wonder why things that are obviously wrong no longer feel wrong. God's established calling is forgotten.

Touch

It is time we become sensitized to all of this. The beginning of sensitization is to feel and be aware of every touch you make. Everything you do be aware of it. It won't drive you crazy; it will make you understand everything around you. Mysteries of the world will soon not be mysteries and lies will soon be seen for what they are, lies. This devotion is not easy but its right.

Through this we will feel again. We will be aware of every touch. Think of a loving relationship or maybe even physical intimacy where we are aware of every small touch. The amazing feeling and love that comes from this purity is intense, real, and passionate.

So give back the barriers and fancy lights and see things in their rawest form. See them as they were created to be seen. The Indians saw the earth differently. Just the same, you can see your intimacy differently.

The Beginning

> Matthew 19: 8
> "But it was not this way from the beginning"

Sensitization is a very tough subject. It brings about many questions. Here was mine. What would it be like if two people were completely sin-less and they were married? What would their physical relationship look like? How would it be different from ours? I have pondered this question for some time. Then it occurred to me that there was a couple that lived and loved together and had relations- and for some time did this completely blame-less.

This was the original relationship between Adam and Eve. There was no bondage of sin when Adam first looked at Eve's naked body. I cannot even fathom what this experience was like for them. What he thought and how he felt towards her. How she felt and what she thought of him. They lived and loved purely together fully sensitized to reality. It wouldn't be going on a limb to say that their physical intimacy probably looked a lot different.

The sin had to be a radical turning point. I think about afterwards when Adam and Eve ran and hid their naked bodies. They hid of course in shame of what they had done- for they did not want God to see them now. Obviously Adam and Eve were so desensitized from sin. So when they sinned, they felt the shame! Imagine when Adam first saw Eve again. The feeling he felt lusting after her. The feeling she felt. He felt awful I'm sure and it had to sadden Eve. Probably the same could be said for Eve looking at Adam. This was a price they had to pay for sin.

While I do not know the rest of the story I would like to imagine Adam fought this lust and tried once again to look at his wife as he did before. I would also like to believe that Eve fought against her fear and guilt and pursued once again a pure relationship with Adam. I will never know how it went, but it is my wish not only that Adam and Eve pursued this purity again, but that in your relationship, you will also.

Chapter 14
The Tryst

The Sensual Act of Intimacy

"Love is the action, decision, and thought of not pleasing yourself but in turn becoming pleased because you didn't."

If this were a physical action, what would it look like? I imagined this for some time. I didn't come out with an answer; I just knew most couldn't be physical and say they loved like this above statement. That most physical intimacy is self gratifying and not about pleasing the other person. That if love was really about pleasing the other person, then I had to change the way I thought about physical intimacy. So that is exactly what I did.

The fullest magnification of love and pleasure in the sensual act of intimacy is when you are there to please the other. Just like the initial stage- the man is there to unconditionally love and please his wife and the woman is there to unconditionally love and please her husband. Together they both strive for the same thing - to please the other. This act of walking together is the fullest magnification of intimacy and will in turn provide the most pleasure. This is worthy to be called, "making love".

Making love is a spiritual term. It cannot be done without intimacy and intimacy cannot be accomplished without God. Intellectually you both love and forgive each other. You fight for the truth of who you both are. You make sure you both acknowledge who you are in Christ and what your relationship is - a life devoted to the glory of God. Through this, you are overflowed with passion and an action occurs. This action is physical intimacy and it is more than sexual intercourse. It is spiritual sexual intercourse where you are sensitized to truly feel everything- To truly see things again and really feel the beauty of each other like you were created to long ago. Spiritual sexual intercourse is what truly binds two together.

The Tryst

A tryst - An assumed designated meeting, freely romantic and without sin - between friend, lover, and Lord. It is out of your control. There will be no idols because your lives will not be like anyone else's. It is a revolution. Your plans, theories, and ideas are thrown away. Your life becomes real.

The word tryst is normally used in a number of fashions. Sometimes you say it is an appointment with another to date, to see one another, sometimes sexually. And usually it refers to an action of your self.

A tryst in spiritual terms I believe is much different. A tryst in spiritual terms is the established perfection that God created us to have in a relationship. Let me tell you what this looks like.

This is where all meetings are appointed by God and ordained by Him. It is a divine appointment by God. You do not idolize movies or stories because you acknowledge your story is different from anyone else's. You give up your own plans, theories, and ideas. You no longer live blinded to the truth- your love, emotion, and passion is real now- your life is real.

A tryst is idealistic, foolish, optimistic, unsuccessful, and illogical. It however is not unbiblical, unreasonable, or impure. A tryst is a beautiful thing.

The Ending

I was in the principles office. Not for punishment, but something much worse.

The principle sat down. With no expression he said,

"Matt you are a popular guy here and we all respect you very much. What I mean is- Although I am not outspoken, I am a Christian. This year you have been asked to head up the baccalaureate service and I have heard a few things."

"What's wrong" I asked.

"Well, this year we want to do some things differently. We want to be accepting to all faiths. Now I personally practice Christianity, but some do not. So we'd like to have a Christian speaker and then also someone from another faith. Do you see where I'm coming from?"

As he finished I stood up and said, "I understand. Let me see what I can do"

"Perfect" he answered "I knew you'd be on board".

Only problem was, I wasn't on board. The principle wanted me to plan an event where a guy would lie and mislead 4000 of my classmates. I had no idea about tolerance or politics or the debates on moral relativism. I just knew this was wrong. So I refused. Friends at school were very upset but I honestly didn't even care. I told my principle and my friends that I loved them, but this is what I'm doing.

So the big night came. The entire class showed up with friends and family. Instead of a Jewish speaker, my youth pastor spoke. He sent around little note cards that night. On them were the letters "DSFSB" written across.

Through Scripture, imagery, and stories he firmly asked us to make a promise. That no matter what we do in life- Don't settle for second best.

If you're a Muslim, become a Christian. If you're dating the wrong person, break up with them. If you're going to the wrong school, transfer. Just whatever you do, don't settle for second best.

This upset many people. Many wanted to be Muslim. Some wanted to date the wrong person. Others just wanted to continue compromising their whole lives. Compromise is a vile and horrid word.

I remember the words even today. Don't settle for second best. Don't trust in success, tolerance, addiction, generic love, your ideas, your choice, or an earthly tryst that will never fulfill you. Trust in God, the right way, forgiveness, true love, His choice, holiness, beauty, and wait for your own perfect spiritual tryst even through all the pain. My friends, whatever you do in life- don't settle for second best.

Contact the Author:
Matt.Henning@uscm.org
Magnify-life.com